dance

2wice

dance

EDITED BY PATSY TARR AND ABBOTT MILLER

TEXTS BY NANCY DALVA

Phaidon Press Limited
Regent's Wharf
All Saints Street
London N1 9PA

Phaidon Press Inc.
180 Varick Street
New York, NY 10014

www.phaidon.com

First published 2004
© 2004 Phaidon Press Limited

ISBN 0 7148 4365 2

A CIP catalogue record of this book is
available from the British Library.

Designed by Abbott Miller, Pentagram
Printed in Hong Kong

CONTENTS

7   DANCE IS EVERYWHERE BY PATSY TARR

9   CHOREO GRAPHIC DESIGN BY ABBOTT MILLER

12   MERCE CUNNINGHAM DANCE COMPANY

20   JAMIE BISHTON

26   MARK MORRIS

30   MARIA CALEGARI AND BART COOK

36   THE PARSONS DANCE COMPANY

44   O VERTIGO

50   PAUL TAYLOR DANCE COMPANY

62   DAVID PARKER AND THE BANG GROUP

68   ALEXANDRE PROIA

72   KAROLE ARMITAGE

78   BALLET BOYZ

82   ROB BESSERER AND MARJORIE FOLKMAN

86   TOM GOLD

94   BANU OGAN

100   PAUL TAYLOR DANCE COMPANY

104   MOLISSA FENLEY

106   ELIZABETH STREB

112   STEPHEN PETRONIO DANCE COMPANY

124   FOOFWA D'IMOBILITÉ

128   ALBERT EVANS AND DANCERS

138   ALEXANDRE PROIA

142   PAUL TAYLOR DANCE COMPANY

152   PETER BOAL

158   APPENDIX

160   INDEX

DANCE
IS
EVERYWHERE

PATSY TARR

Twyla Tharp and the original company of her Broadway production of Movin' Out, from the "Camera" (Spring 2001) issue of 2wice, photographed by Martin Schoeller. Left to right: Keith Roberts, Twyla Tharp, Benjamin Bowman, Elizabeth Parkinson, Ashley Tuttle, and John Selya.

The relationship between moving — or not-moving — people and their surroundings always occupies my mind. (I am continually moving the furniture around in my apartment, trying to find the perfect relationship between people and objects.) This sensibility became the framework for 2wice magazine, informing every issue.

After many years spent attending dance concerts, I realized that the way I saw the world had changed. I saw everything through a choreographic lens: weddings, funerals, checkout lines, subway riders, elevator passengers, partygoers. All human activity seemed to express an informal organization approaching a real choreographic effort. A large space with moving masses of people came to fascinate me, as did a small space with stationary inhabitants. I loved, and still do, the swirl of humanity in the Great Hall of the Metropolitan Museum of Art in Manhattan, the static arrangement and spacing of individuals in the reading room of the New York Public Library. I'm dazzled by the rush of runners crossing the Brooklyn Bridge during the marathon.

The pages of 2wice magazine attempt to interpret the world in a visually kinetic way. We try to establish new ways of seeing; to make new connections; to set up new correspondences. We try to see ourselves in scale with the world. Thus we examine the ways we live, and the artifacts with which we live. The broad avenues of our inquiries intersect on issues of the body: movement, fashion, the representations we make of ourselves and of others. The choreographers and dancers on these pages became our partners in communicating our ideas; and we, in turn, in communicating theirs. The pictures are collaborations between the artists and the photographers and 2wice. They are a performance.

CHOREO GRAPHIC DESIGN

ABBOTT MILLER

Photography and cover design from the "Rites of Spring" (Spring 2000) issue of 2wice, featuring Foofwa d'Imobilité, in a costume of his own design, photographed by Martin Schoeller.

Over the last several years 2wice magazine has explored the relationship between dance and photography by working with some of the most talented choreographers and photographers to create a unique publication. We conceived 2wice as an alternative venue for performance, one that had the added virtue of becoming a lasting, physical record of an evanescent art form. 2wice has sought to document dancers and choreographers in ways that acknowledge the interplay between the performer and the photographer. Rather than attempt to capture signature choreographic movements, the goal has been to conceive of the shoot itself as a two-sided performance, a duet between the photographer and his or her subject.

Published biannually for the last seven years, 2wice has taken on a broad range of themes in its exploration of performance, photography, and design. Our approach to the magazine has been to think of photography, design, and text as an ensemble of parts. We begin each issue with a theme or key word whose associations and tangents allow us to develop a visual and editorial framework.

Our themes have been both extremely specific — such as UNIFORM or PICNIC — and deliberately abstract, such as GLOW, allowing us to make connections between the visual and performing arts. While dance is the core of 2wice's identity, it has been our goal to present it within the broader context of the visual arts. This cross-disciplinary perspective grows directly out of the hybrid nature of dance: It is a truly multimedia art form, embracing music and sound, costume, and stage design. Hence 2wice's recurring interest in clothing and costume, design, photography and art, literary artifacts, and other aspects of the visual arts.

Over the years 2wice has often been described as feeling more like a book than a magazine, a remark we have always taken as a compliment. Revisiting our favorite photographs to create Dance 2wice seems both natural and inevitable. We thank the photographers and performers with whom we have worked over the years for allowing us to present their images in this new context.

THE PERFORMANCES

Merce Cunningham Dance Company

Merce Cunningham's "Events" bring together elements of complete dances, excerpts from the company's repertory, and new sequences arranged for a particular time and place. They often create a landscape in which different activities are happening at the same time, allowing for what Cunningham describes as "not so much a dance as the experience of dance."

When this old world starts getting me down and people are just too much for me to face, I climb way up to the top of the stairs, and all my cares just drift right into space....

In the many years since Merce Cunningham moved his enterprise to the top floor of Westbeth, a big, blocky apartment building on the corner of Bethune and West Streets in lower Manhattan, his dancers have lived the usual studio life, augmented by a kind of ongoing offhand picnic. Their *vie bohème* has been enhanced by the adjacent rooftop, where they can sneak off to eat lunch, smoke, gossip, or catch a breeze off the Hudson River.

On July 24, 2001, we went out on the roof with Cunningham and his company for a dance event staged specifically for the camera, with the choreographer devising a canny cross between Statues and Simon Says. First he set his dancers in motion— using excerpts from his repertory—then he froze them for the camera. This was different from the usual caught-in-the-act dance photography; this was a careful, composed collaboration between the choreographer and the photographer, Christian Witkin. From time to time as the afternoon got hotter and hotter, the dancers retreated to the dressing room to change from one fanciful summer outfit to another. The sky blazed blue as blue, but they stayed cool as cucumbers, up on their roof.

On the roof, the only place I know where you just have to wish to make it so...

In mid-September, the contact sheets came back. In the foreground, dancers. In the background, the Twin Towers of the World Trade Center. Up on the roof that afternoon, we captured time.

Let me tell you now—when I come home all tired and beat, I go up where the air is fresh and sweet...

We went to talk to Merce. One would think, we said, that people would move on, and buildings would stay. "But they didn't," he replied. "Did they?" For a lifetime, he has made dances that reflect nature and people. They vanished even as they were happening. Dance is the evanescent art form, all tempus fugit and now, it would seem, memento mori.

Right smack-dab in the middle of town I've found a paradise that's trouble free...

"Everything is changed now," said Merce.

And if this world starts getting you down there's room enough for two up on the roof...

We were in Eden then, but we didn't know it.

Up on the roof. Oh, come on baby. Come on honey. Everything is all right.

In mid-October, Merce was upstairs at Westbeth, talking with visitors. For fifty years, dancers have repeated his trenchant remark to an early member of the company: "The only way to do it is to do it." That afternoon, resolute and wistful, he was heard to say this: "We can only do what we can do."

Oh we gotta go up on the roof.

Jamie Bishton

Manet's Le Déjeuner sur l'herbe is art history's iconic picnic. All of classicism leads up to it; all of modernism leads away. Shocking in its day—which was the mid-nineteenth century—the Déjeuner has retained its provocative character all through the years. From the outset, much has been made about the lone nude figure in the scene, which was painted in the artist's studio. What seems to matter is not so much that she is naked but that no one else is. This leads to a strange imbalance of power, but it is hard to say—though art critics have made a lot of stabs at it—exactly how the scales are tipped. Here, in the grand tradition of reinterpretations, choreographer Jamie Bishton, in league with photographer Tony Rinaldo, stages his own recensions in the real outdoors.

PHOTOGRAPHER: MARTIN SCHOELLER

Mark Morris

He is a flower child,
he is the American flag,
he is a gentleman
caller in flip-flops.
He is going to swig a beer,
sip a mint julep,
hit the boardwalk.
He's from the East Coast,
and he's from the East.
He's Dorothy's brother
on his way across a
field of daisies
to see the Wizard of Oz.
He's a gingham wolf on his way
to intercept Little Red
Riding Hood. (For that he's
certainly charming enough.)
She'd probably hand her
wicker hamper right over.
"Mmmm," the wolf is thinking.
"Lamb chops."
Whatever he is, Mark Morris
isn't just your ordinary
picnic god, your everyday
Bacchus in Gingham.
Mark Morris is a feast.

Maria Calegari and Bart Cook

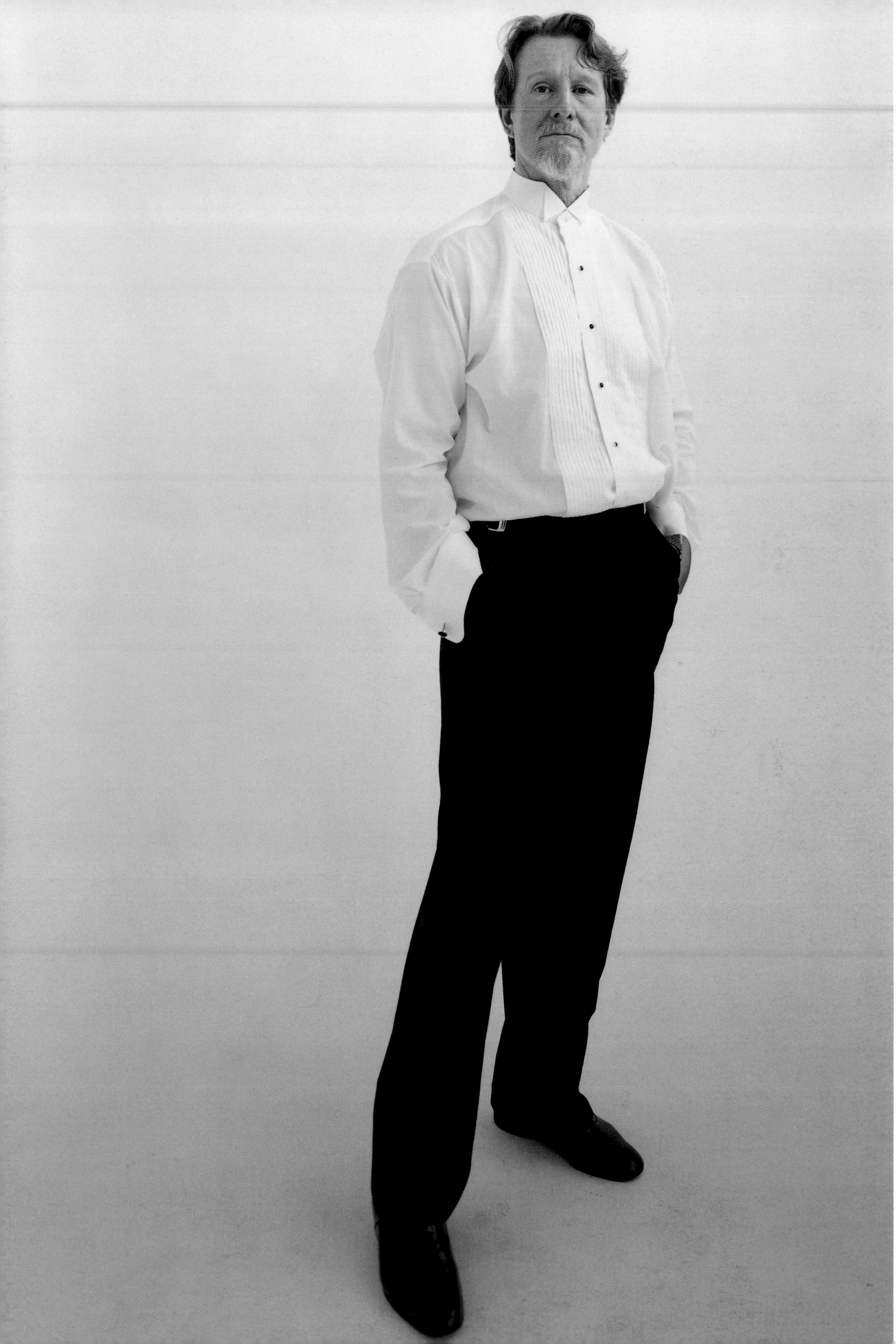

PHOTOGRAPHER: CHRISTIAN WITKIN

I dreamt I went skating.... David Parsons and the dancers of the Parsons Dance Company collaborate with photographer Martin Schoeller on the notion of animal, together devising this snowy landscape where the naked are warm, as in a Norse night kitchen. Are these ice people or just you and me, powdered in sleepy dust? What is this darkling creature who creeps among us, eyes aglow? Benign? Malign? Predator? Protector? Make of him what you will, whenever your eyes close, his open. Aprowl between conscious and subconscious, waking and sleeping, he's the man of our dreams.

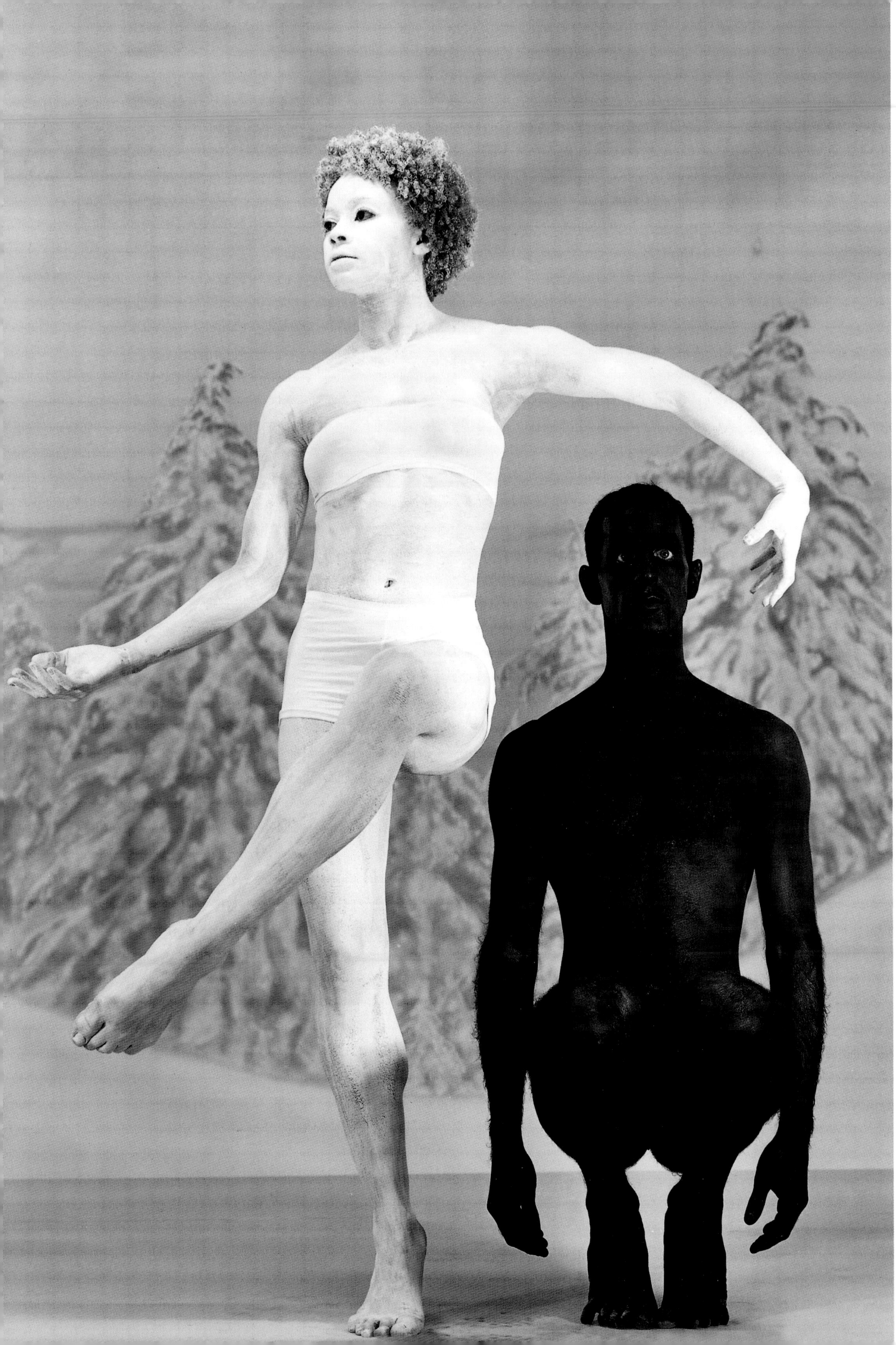

PHOTOGRAPHER: MARTIN SCHOELLER

O Vertigo

PHOTOGRAPHER: JOANNE SAVIO

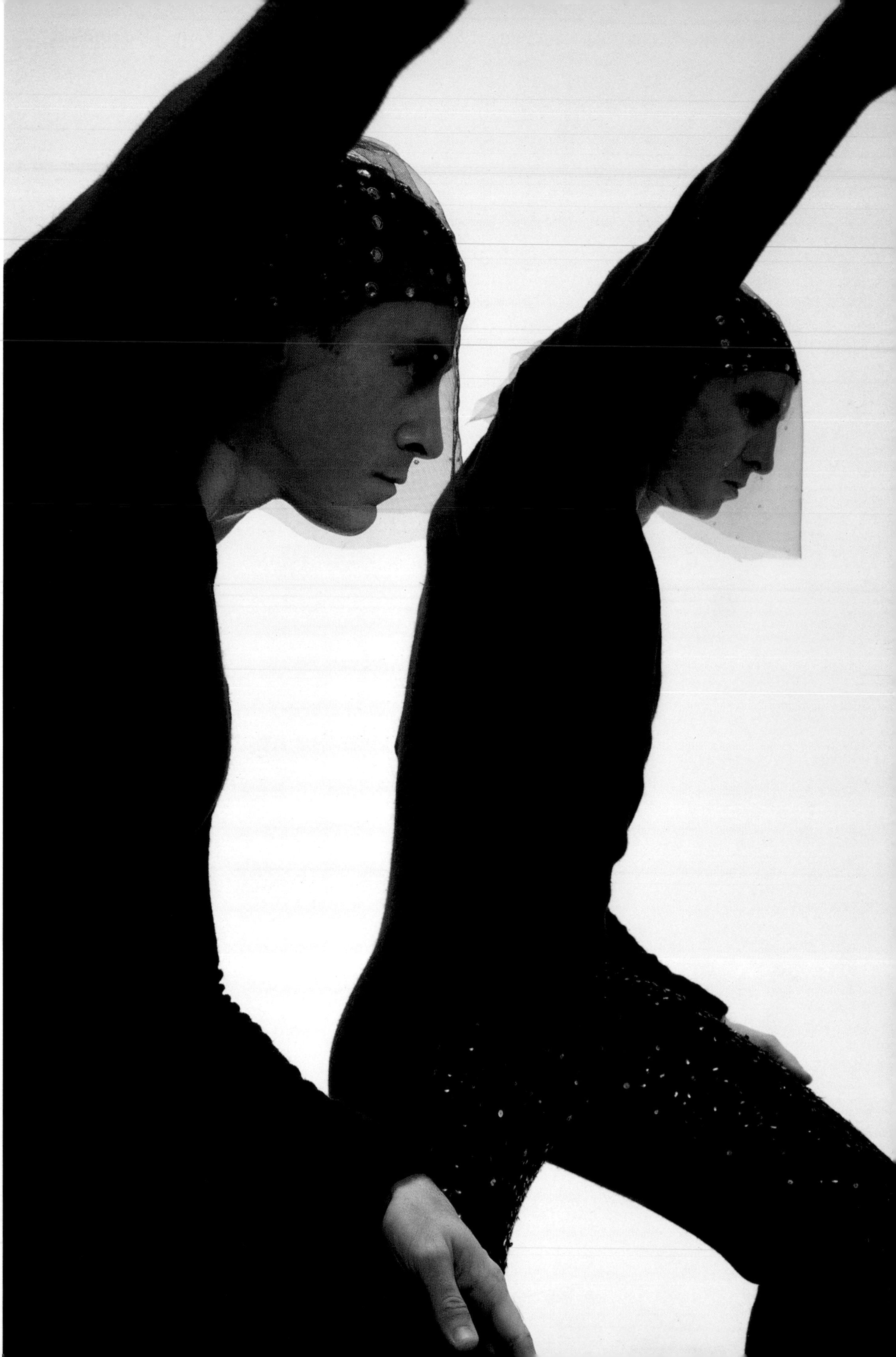

PHOTOGRAPHER: ANDREW ECCLES

Lost, Found, Lost (shown here in modified excerpts). Made by Paul Taylor in 1982 using material from *Seven Dances* (1957), about which he later would write: "Lines of restless people at banks, theaters, and rest rooms. Wads crammed into elevators or spaced artistically on subway platforms or leaning against skyscrapers. They are standing, squatting, sitting everywhere like marvelous bees or ants, and their moves and stillnesses are ABCs that if given a proper format could define dance in a new way."

Costumes by Alex Katz, unisex. Pop music from the 1940s, when Taylor was a waiter in a restaurant that played background music. Then and now: hep and hip. Gesture equals posture, and vice versa.

Less is more. Cool, cooler, coolest.

PHOTOGRAPHER: CHRISTIAN WITKIN

David Parker and the Bang Group

In the postmodern dance world, where the parade of the unmediated self is a constant, David Parker—pictured here with his company, the Bang Group—is ironic yet insistent. He has an abiding faith in the intrinsic musicality of the body as its own instrumental accompanist, of its potential as a percussion instrument, of its ability to stand—or tap—on its own. He is in fact a purist, albeit one swathed in bubble wrap, which Parker likes, of course, for its alluring aural possibilities: "Let's talk noise. I'm all for that. Noise in dance is associated with lowbrow dance; and silence, with highbrow dance. I like mixtures of those: quiet tap dancing, loud pointe work, stomping dances to classical music, and lyrical dances to 'Bei Mir Bist Du Schön.' I'm very interested in making work that uses rhythm to create a physical syntax that has the clarity and immediacy of speech."

Alexandre Proia

In this interpretation for 2wice of Nijinsky's L'Après-Midi d'un Faune, a work that has spawned many imitators and interpreters, Alexandre Proia conjures the dance — about a satyr intoxicated by a nymph, whose scarf is attainable, if she is not — entire. By appropriating the maidenly garment as his own, Proia becomes at once the desired and the desirer, the dressed and the undressed, the instinctual and the contrived, the male and the female. He's your postmodern faun: all and everything, in a sarong.

Karole Armitage

Choreographer Karole Armitage has been billed, notably, as the "Punk Ballerina" and the "Wild Ballerina." She has danced in wildly divergent circumstances: in rock videos for Madonna and Michael Jackson; in films, including The Golden Bowl; in the Merce Cunningham Dance Company, where she was a modernina rather than a ballerina; and in George Balanchine's Geneva Ballet. A high-kicking take-no-prisoners blonde, Armitage is possessed of a radical cool allied with true, unalloyed oomph. But the punk and the wild are misleading. They have something to do with edgy hair, fashiony costumes, and the high-volume music she has sometimes favored. They have nothing to do with the leggy, ineradicable, bred-in-the-bone glamour that underpins everything she takes on, or puts on.

Ballet Boyz

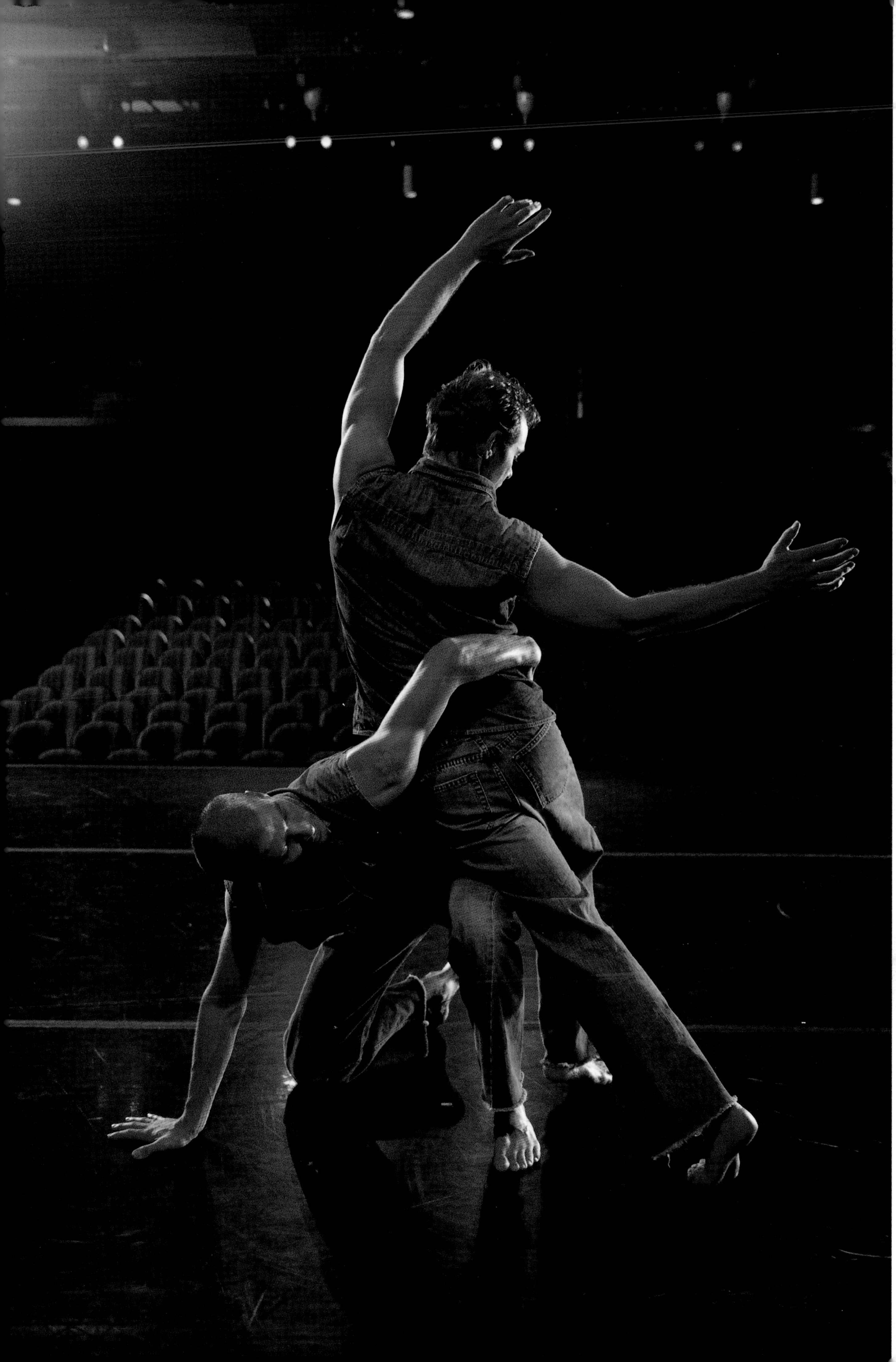

PHOTOGRAPHER: CHRISTIAN WITKIN

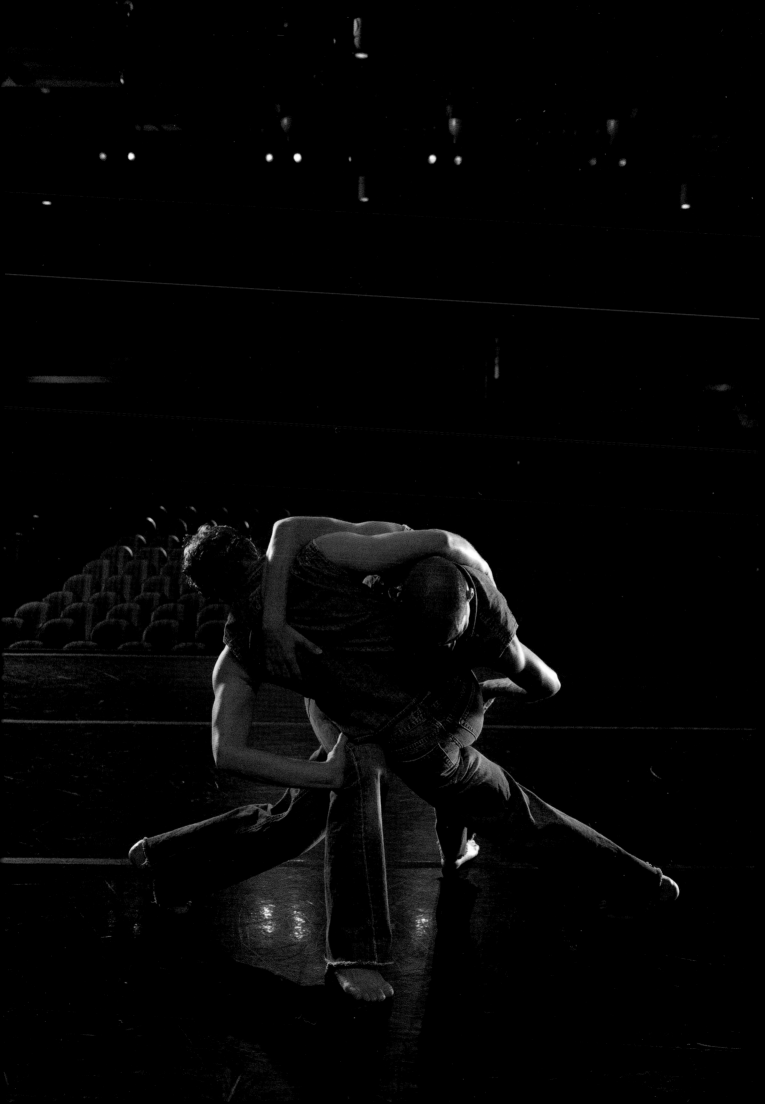

Rob Besserer and Marjorie Folkman

fig. 1

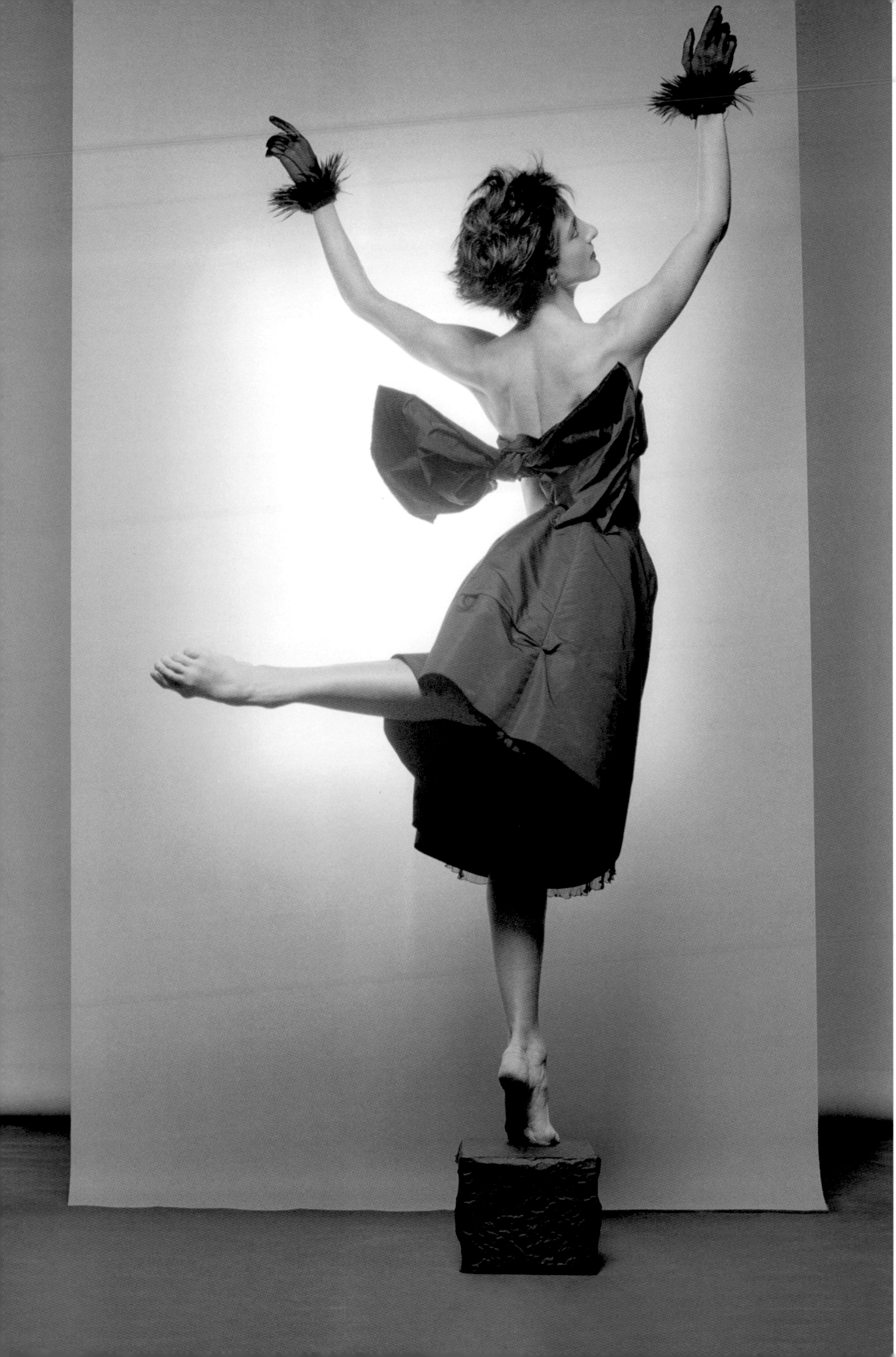

PHOTOGRAPHER: JOSEF ASTOR

New York City Ballet soloist Tom Gold: quicksilver, eager, and versatile, he dances Balanchine, Robbins, Tharp; Martins, Forsythe, Tanner. He is the incarnation of Mercury, the messenger of the gods, carrying a news flash from Terpsichore, the muse of dance: Classicism is as modern as you can get.

PHOTOGRAPHER: ANDREW ECCLES

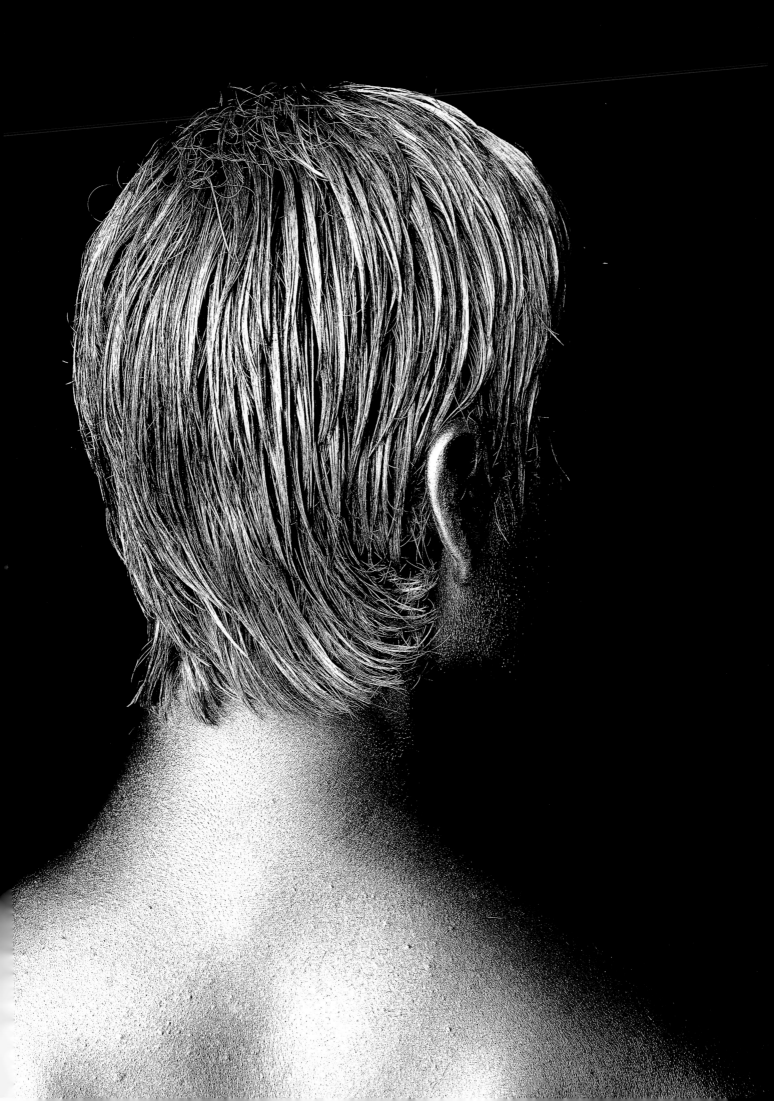

Banu Ogan: born in Ankara, Turkey; grew up in Bloomington, Indiana; holds a degree in biology; member of the Merce Cunningham Dance Company from spring 1993 to summer 2000. Languorous and art historical in the Cunningham repertory, where her out-of-the-seraglio beauty mesmerized her audience and flattered her partners. Out on her own, a postmodern Modigliani. Even when dancing on ice, Banu keeps her cool.

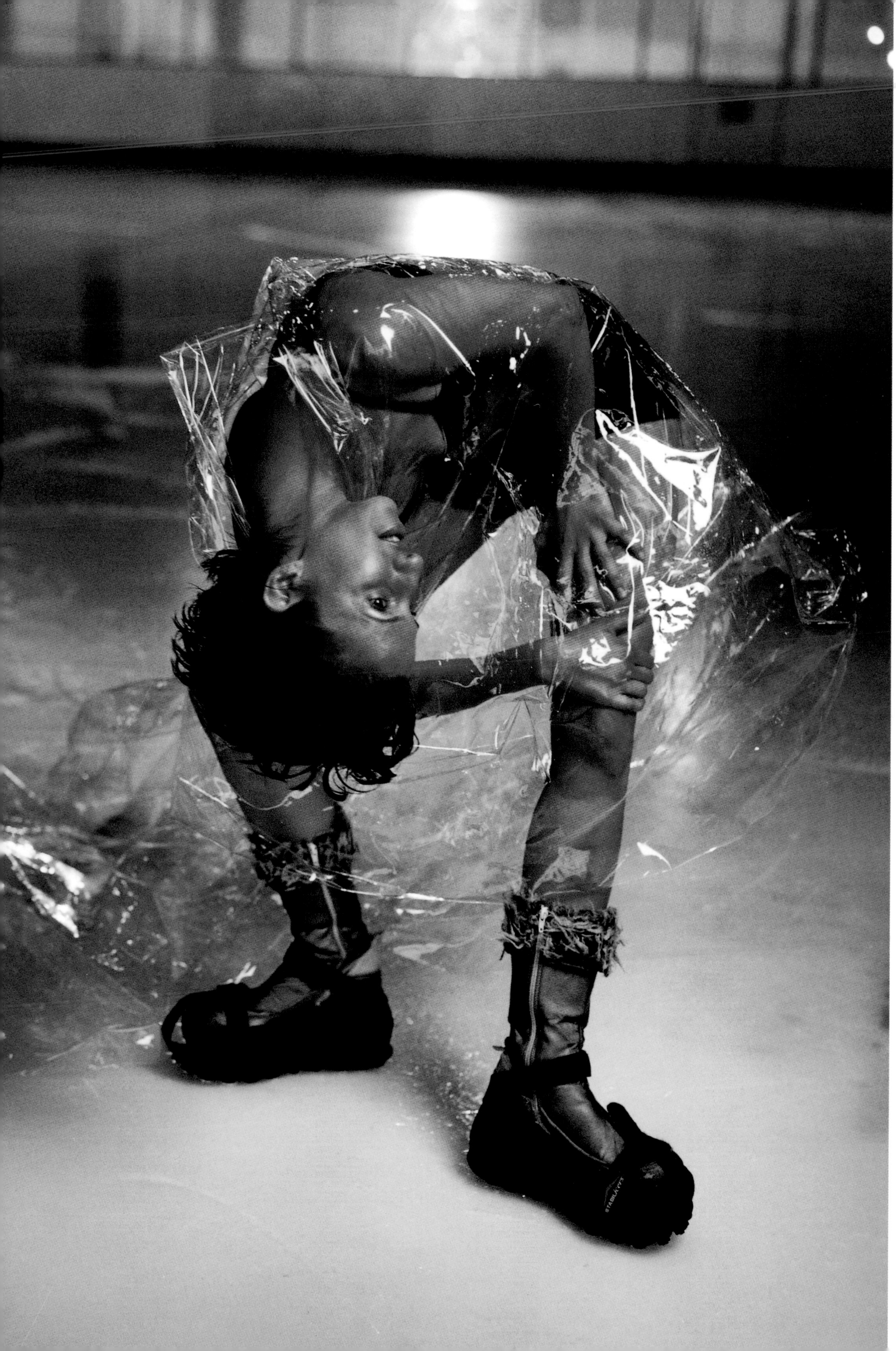

PHOTOGRAPHER: ANDERS OVERGAARD

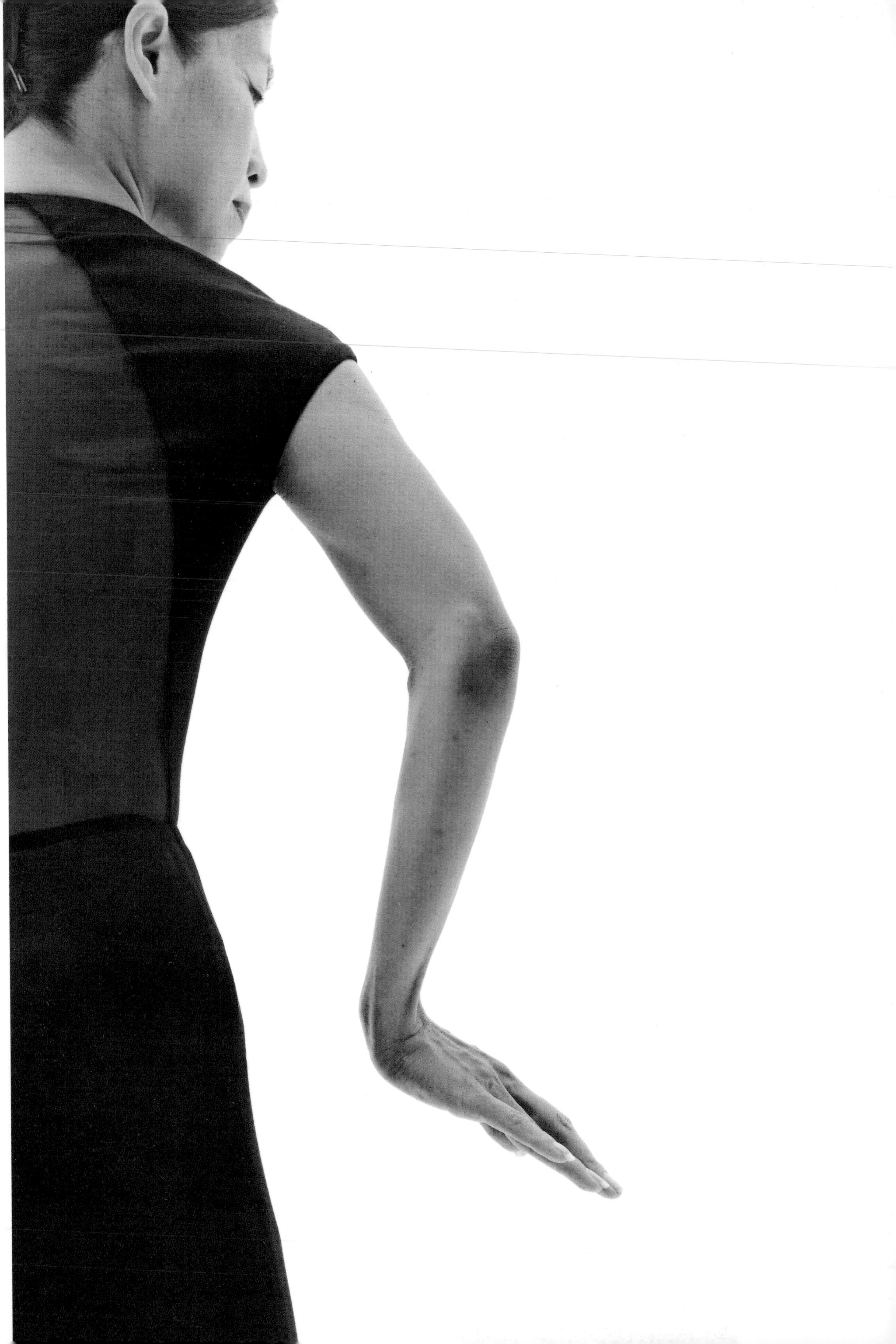

PHOTOGRAPHER: CHRISTIAN WITKIN

Molissa Fenley

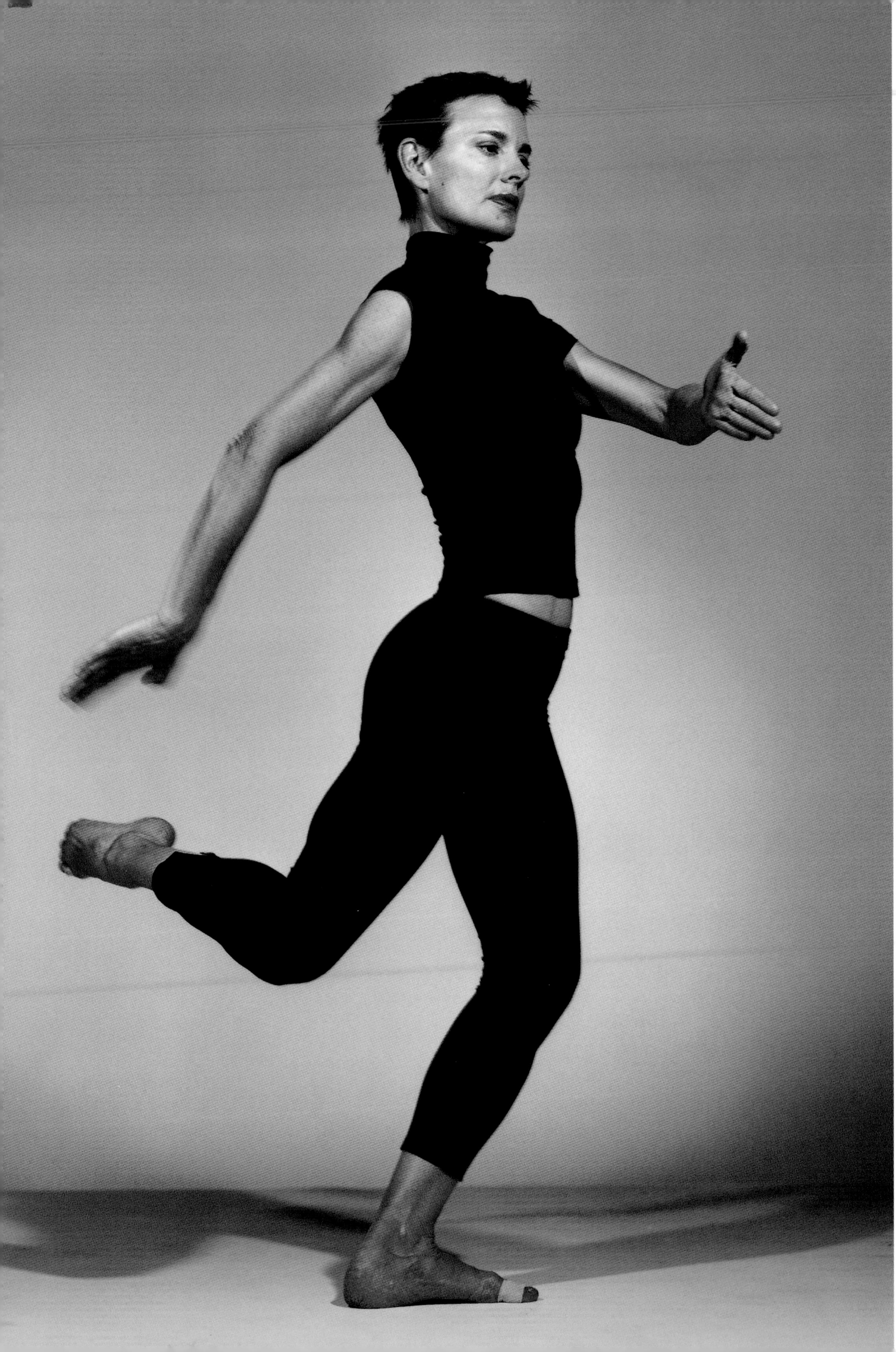

PHOTOGRAPHER: MARTIN SCHOELLER

Elizabeth Streb

The box is a perfect little theater, and, as the woman in the box says, "In the theater it is always night." What time of night? "The millisecond you are in," she says, but she means the millisecond she is in. We are simply in it with her, in this millisecond that belongs so compellingly to her, all the light, all the air, all the thought. "If you are really physically present," she says, "directionality in time disappears. You are not awake in the normal sense, in the box. You are in the continuous present." And that, exactly, is where *Little Ease* resides now — in the mind's eye, and in the camera's. For fourteen years, this was Elizabeth Streb's galvanic signature piece, the one she kept at after easing out of all her other work and leaving the dancing to her company, called STREB. Her final performance was in her studio. You see it here…. Many people think the box is a coffin. "Really?" she asks. Or is the box the body, and the dancer the unquiet mind within, visited and revisited by what it least wants to contemplate? Isn't having little ease a bad thing? "No, no," she says. "To me ease is the enemy. I fail if I care about missing a move or if a previous move doesn't force me into another with no second thoughts, no care about outcome, people, places, times, things. I fail if urgency disappears. I fail if I don't use myself up totally — to be here! and there! and over there!"

When he made his solo Broken Man, Stephen Petronio was recovering from a broken foot. He appears to have fallen out of something at high velocity — a vehicle, a thought, a happiness, his clothes. (This breakaway moment is mirrored by the rising, fringe-clad Ashleigh Leite in City of Twist.) The Petronio Dance Company currently traverses the divide facing all performer-choreographers, where the power of the mind begins to exceed the power of the body, and the choreographer's thoughts are made manifest in the movement of others. Petronio's foot is mended, but what about his ever-fashionable heart?

Stephen Petronio Dance Company

Foofwa d'Imobilité

Foofwa d'Imobilité was born in Geneva to dancer and teacher Beatriz Consuelo and photographer Claude Gafner and until several years ago was known as Frédéric Gafner. Under that name he studied at the École de Danse and the Ballet Junior and was recognized at the Prix de Lausanne and other dance competitions for his technical purity and classical style. From 1987 to 1990, he danced in the corps de ballet of the Stuttgart Ballet and was already dancing soloist roles when he became interested in the modern complexities of Merce Cunningham. Leaving Europe behind for a time, he came to New York City to dance with the Merce Cunningham Dance Company for seven exceptional years. His ability to jump, his extreme clarity, and his ability to cut the air into facets reminded many of Cunningham in his own performing days, and Cunningham made many significant roles for him. In 1995, he won the New York Dance and Performance Award (Bessie) for "exceptional creative achievement in the work of Merce Cunningham." Toward the end of his time with the company, Frédéric morphed into Foofwa, reminding some of Dada papa Marcel Duchamp's double life as Rrose Sélavy. Working from the transliterated French—Fou Fois—the name can be translated as "Crazy When Not Moving." He has gone on to a career as a solo multimedia artist, presenting work in New York, Paris, Brussels, The Hague, Geneva, and Cologne, incorporating his own texts and video in his performances. He is known to his friends as Foof.

Albert Evans and Dancers

Ballet is a formal language, with an alphabet of positions and steps, which can vary from country to country, company to company, school to school. Choreographers, especially great ones, also have their own distinctive styles. The dancers you see here, for example, all speak fluent Balanchine. All dance in the company he founded, the New York City Ballet. Here, though, they are speaking something new, as Albert Evans, a NYCB principal, steps out on his own as a choreographer, and Janie Taylor and Sébastien Marcovici join him in a classical conversation devised for us.

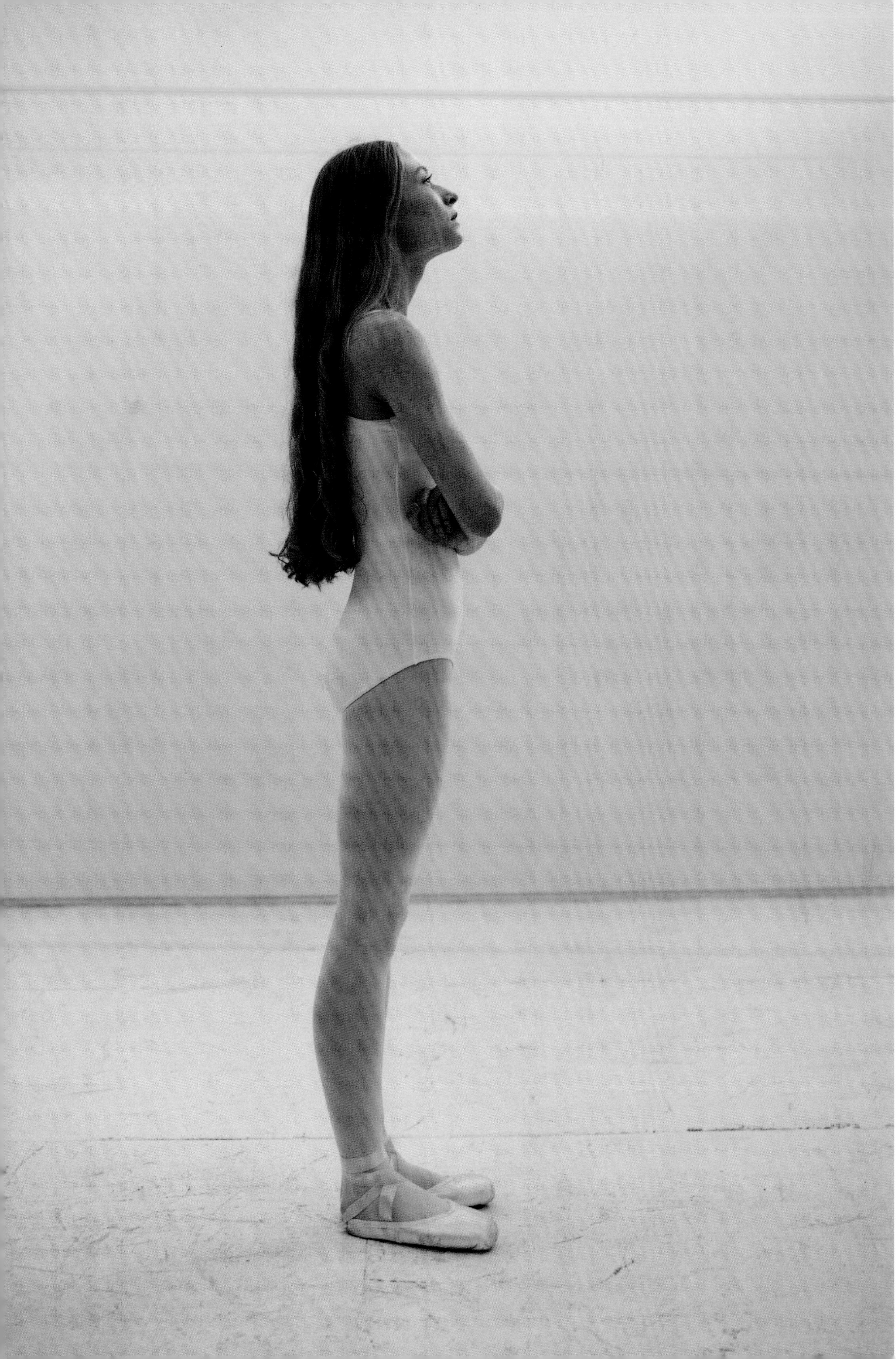

PHOTOGRAPHER: CHRISTIAN WITKIN

Alexandre Proia

PHOTOGRAPHER: MARTIN SCHOELLER

PHOTOGRAPHER: CHRISTIAN WITKIN

Cloven Kingdom, seen in a studio performance. Choreographed in 1976 by Paul Taylor, who quotes Spinoza in a program note: "Man is a social animal." Deeply rooted in the divided nature of humans. (What goes better with tails than paws?) A glinting, transformative version of the rite of spring known as prom night. (And not Taylor's first. At the Virginia Episcopal School in Lynchburg, he headed the hop committee.) Taylor is a habitual observer of animal behavior. He is a dog lover. He is a butterfly collector. Insects fascinate him. (Jitter! Bug!) People, too, he knows well, although we perhaps appeal to him less, given as we are to various deceptions unknown in the lower kingdoms. (Animals may perform, but they don't rehearse, or theorize.) Yet Taylor loves the lies that make up art and tells them well. (Isn't that the truth?) You would think a man in formal attire, at a dance, would be engaged in the most civilized, the least animal, of activities. But as you can see, Taylor knows better.

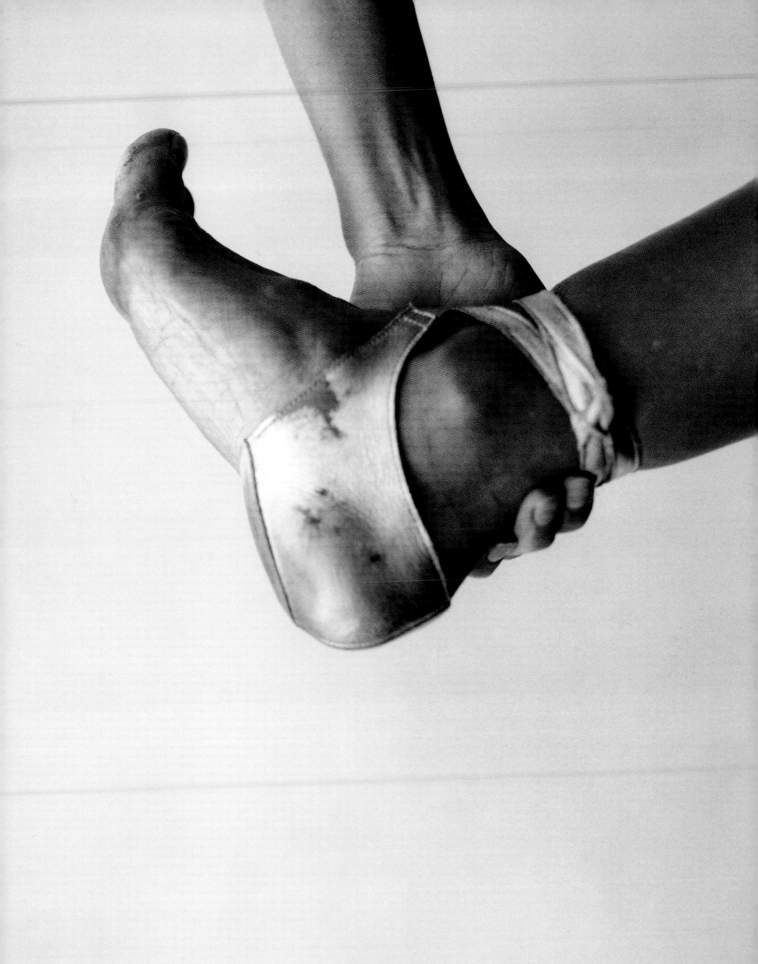

PHOTOGRAPHER: CHRISTIAN WITKIN

Choreographer Wendy Perron's The Man and the Echo is a study—a kind of portrait, but one that delves beneath the surface—of and for the dancer Peter Boal. In the theater (and in these photos) you see the signature calligraphic gestures of a postmodernist drawn by a bred-in-the-bone classicist. As a principal with the New York City Ballet and a teacher for the School of American Ballet, Boal defines the danseur noble. He is a prince, a god, a king. But here—dressed in that most pedestrian of garments, a business suit— he's a renegade. (Perron has broken in, Boal has broken out.) This dance fits him like a second skin, to get underneath yours.

KAROLE ARMITAGE formed Armitage Gone! Dance in 1979 while still a member of the Merce Cunningham Dance Company. She merges her classical training, her background dancing for George Balanchine in the Ballet du Grand Théâtre de Genève, and her six years with Cunningham into an edgy approach that has earned her the nickname "Punk Ballerina." The former director of the Ballet of Florence, MaggioDanza, she alternates guest commissions, choreographing for the Ballet de Lorraine in Nancy, France, and making dances for her own company. She collaborates extensively with artists in other fields.

The BALLET BOYZ now derive their name from their very popular television diaries, made while they were with Britain's Royal Ballet, where they danced for twelve years. Michael Nunn and William Trevitt first founded their London-based troupe as George Piper Dances (these being their middle names). Although they intersperse their performances with amusing filmed self-documentaries, they are serious and brilliant classical technicians who collaborate with notable contemporary choreographers, such as Russell Maliphant, to bring ballet-based dancing vividly into the present day. Featured dancers, pages 78–81: Michael Nunn, William Trevitt

ROB BESSERER and MARJORIE FOLKMAN are dancer's dancers. He has danced notably for Lar Lubovitch, Baryshnikov's White Oak Dance Project, Martha Clarke, and Mark Morris, among others. He is also an actor. She is a noted dance researcher and a member of the Mark Morris Dance Group.

JAMIE BISHTON danced with distinction for the American Ballet Theatre from 1988 to 1990 and for Twyla Tharp from 1985 through 1999. He was an original member of Mikhail Baryshnikov's White Oak Dance Project before founding his own elegant eponymous troupe, Jamie Bishton Dance, in 2003. Featured dancers, pages 20–25: Jamie Bishton, Ashleigh Leite, Ana Gonzalez, Andrew Robinson

PETER BOAL, widely regarded as the ultimate danseur noble, has spent his career with the New York City Ballet, since 1989 as a principal dancer. He now serves on the faculty of School of American Ballet, where he trained as a boy. A frequent guest artist, he has recently formed Peter Boal & Company, a trio that will acquire works that blur the line between classical and modern dance. He has also performed a commissioned program of contemporary solos.

MARIA CALEGARI and BART COOK were principal dancers for the New York City Ballet, where Cook was also an assistant ballet master. They are both repetiteurs for the George Balanchine Trust, and Cook also stages the works of Jerome Robbins and is a choreographer in his own right. Calegari teaches widely and has her own ballet school in Connecticut.

ALBERT EVANS is a choreographer who is a principal dancer for the New York City Ballet, where his work has been presented in the Diamond Project. He is an accomplished interpreter of Balanchine roles, and has also created roles in new works. JANIE TAYLOR and SÉBASTIEN MARCOVICI are soloist and principal, respectively, for the same company. She trained at the School of American Ballet, and he at the School of the Paris Ballet, and then with Jean-Pierre Bonnefoux and Patricia McBride. Featured dancers, pages 128–137: Albert Evans, Sébastien Marcovici, Janie Taylor

MOLISSA FENLEY is known as a solo performer creating in collaboration with visual artists and composers and as a choreographer with her own ensemble, Molissa Fenley and Dancers. Her dances are in the repertories of major companies around the world; her frequent commissions also include work for universities and individuals. She is a master teacher at her alma mater, Mills College, in California.

FOOFWA D'IMOBILITÉ was formerly known as Frédéric Gafner. Working in a "neo-post" style of his own devising, the intellectually inclined Swiss-born danseur subsumes both his classical ballet training and his signal accomplishments dancing with the Merce Cunningham Dance Company in solo and group work and dance videos. He is based in Geneva.

TOM GOLD is a soloist with the New York City Ballet, where he has also been appointed artist-in-residence with the costume department. He has toured with Tharp! and the Donald Byrd Group and studies design at the Fashion Institute of Technology in New York.

The MERCE CUNNINGHAM DANCE COMPANY was founded in 1953 and continues to this day as the vehicle for the modernist iconoclast noted for the separation of dance from music and decor; an original technique that makes possible his style; the introduction of a 360-degree "front" into traditional proscenium theaters; the fragmentation of stage space; the introduction of chance procedures into the choreographic process; the commissioning of scores and scenery from many of his contemporaries; and some fifty years of collaboration with the composer John Cage. His embrace of technology has led him to work in film, in video, with motion capture, and to choreographing by means of a computer program initially known as "Life Forms." His company and school are based at Westbeth, in New York City. Featured dancers, pages 12–19: Cedric Andrieux, Jonah Bokaer, Lisa Boudreau, Ashley Chen, Paige Cunningham, Holley Farmer, Jean Freebury, Jennifer Goggans, Mandy Kirschner, Koji Minato, Daniel Roberts, Daniel Squire, Jeannie Steele, Derry Swan, Robert Swinston, Cheryl Therrien

MARK MORRIS began dancing spontaneously at the age of two, for his appreciative and musical mother. He founded first a company, the Mark Morris Dance Group (in 1980), and then a school (in 1996), located in a custom-built dance center in Brooklyn, New York. His post-modern work is internationalist and humanist, with a global embrace of styles and forms and body types and a similarly wide-ranging musical imperative. All of his choreography is based on and closely (yet with wild invention) interprets the scores to which he sets it; company performances invariably have distinguished live accompaniment. Morris also works widely in ballet and opera. He still performs with his group in a few ensemble pieces, and in solos celebrated for their surpassing stagecraft.

O VERTIGO is based in Montreal, Quebec, and has toured in the United States, Europe, Brazil, Mexico, Israel, and Japan. It is devoted to presenting the work of its founder and artistic director, Ginette Laurin. Her company takes its name from the notion that "Creation is a vertiginous thing; an artist is always at risk of having his body and his heart shattered; of causing turmoil to his senses and emotions." Featured dancer, pages 44–49: Anna Riede

BANU OGAN danced with the Merce Cunningham Dance Company from 1993 to 2000 and has since set or co-set Cunningham's dances on companies in Europe and the United States. She has taught in Switzerland, Turkey, Japan, Spain, and Italy and also performed in the work of Foofwa d'Imobilité and Ashley Chen.

DAVID PARKER and **THE BANG GROUP**, including Kathyrn Tufano and Jeffrey Kazin, are a rhythm-based theatrical dance troupe serving Parker's intelligent fascination with the percussive possibilities of the dancing body. The work is wide-rangingly anarchic and subversive but based on an abiding love of formalism. Featured dancers, pages 62–67: David Parker, Jeffrey Kazin, Kathryn Tufano

THE PARSONS DANCE COMPANY maintains a repertory of over sixty works, some to commissioned scores. After dancing for Paul Taylor from 1978 to 1987, David Parsons founded the troupe, known for their verve and polish, their community-based residencies, and their master classes. Company members are encouraged to choreograph. Their home base is on Forty-second Street in New York. Featured dancers, pages 36–43: David Parsons, Timothy Bish, Elizabeth Koeppen, Marty Lawson, Brian McGinnis, Sumayah McRae, Mia McSwain, Abby Silva, Katarzyna Skarpetowska, Michael Snipe

The **PAUL TAYLOR DANCE COMPANY** has for more than forty years performed Taylor's dances in more than 450 cities in sixty countries. Dark of mind but light of foot, the choreographer fills his hierarchical stage canvases with sculptural, emotionally resonant choreography that marks him as the true heir of Martha Graham, for whom he danced before setting out on his own sui generis journey. Taylor's dances, like his autobiography, *Private Domain*, are fabulist concoctions marked alternately by darkness and light, wicked humor, telling incident, acute observation, and inspired lies that always tell the truth. Featured dancers, pages 50–61: Patrick Corbin, Kristi Egtvedt, Silvia Nevjinsky, Andy LeBeau, Annmaria Mazzini; pages 100–103: Heather Berest, Caryn

Heilman, Maureen Mansfield, Francie Huber, Lisa Viola; pages 142–151: Kristi Egtvedt, Robert Kleinendorst, Andy LeBeau, Silvia Nevjinsky, Julie Tice, Michael Trusnovec, Takehiro Ueyama, Amy Young

ALEXANDRE PROIA began the Proia Dance Theatre to perform his work, which layers "slices of life with abstract images." His dances have been performed by the School of American Ballet, the New York City Ballet, and the School of the Paris Opera Ballet, where he trained. He has appeared with companies including the Boston Ballet and the New York City Ballet; on Broadway; in television and film; and in works by Robert Wilson and Martha Clarke.

The **STEPHEN PETRONIO DANCE COMPANY** derives its name and style from its founder. A tremendously intense performer, he was the first male member of the Trisha Brown Dance Company. For twenty years, Petronio's collaborations with contemporary composers, artists, and fashion designers have lent his work depth and gloss. Recently, his plotless dances have been amplified by vivid emotional subtexts. Featured dancers, pages 112–123: Stephen Petronio, Michael Badger, Gerald Casel, Thang Dao, Gino Grenek, Ashleigh Leite, Jimena Paz, Stephen Petronio, Shila Tirabassi, Amanda Wells

ELIZABETH STREB is the founder of an equipment-based (trampolines, climbing harnesses, bungee cords, portable walls, etc.), readily accessible crossover movement form she calls Pop Action. She eschews pretense, decorative gesture, story, the proscenium, and the trappings of art theater in favor of an ongoing, visceral, danger-courting, love-hate relationship with gravity. STREB, the touring company she formed in 1979, is at home in the Streb Action Invention Lab in Brooklyn, New York.

TWYLA THARP deploys an idiosyncratic style blending elements of the classical and the vernacular into a distinctive amalgam. Since 1965 she has choreographed more than 130 dances for her own companies (the Twyla Tharp Dance Company, Tharp! etc.) and for major ballet companies around the world. She works to music from Bach to Jelly Roll Morton to Bruce Springsteen. Her work on Broadway includes the all-dance musical *Movin' Out*, which she conceived, directed, and choreographed to music by Billy Joel and which won a Tony Award in 2003. She collaborated with Milos Forman on the films *Hair*, *Amadeus*, and *Ragtime*, and for television she directed *Baryshnikov by Tharp*, which won two Emmy Awards. She is the author of two books, *Push Comes To Shove* (an autobiography) and *How to Be Creative*. She lives and works in New York.

Index

Pages with photographs are in gray only after the photographer's entry ("photographs by").

Armitage, Karole, 72–77, 158
Astor, Josef, photographs by, 82–84

Balanchine, George, 73, 86, 128
Ballet Boyz, 78–81, 158
Ballet Junior, 124
Bang Group, the, 62–67
"Bei Mir Bist Du Schön," 63
Besserer, Rob, 82–84, 158
Bishton, Jamie, 20–25, 158
Boal, Peter, 152–57, 158
Bowman, Benjamin, 6
Broken Man (Petronio), 113

Calegari, Maria, 30–35, 158
City of Twist (Petronio), 113
Cloven Kingdom (Taylor), 142
Consuelo, Beatriz, 124
Cook, Bart, 31–35, 158
Cunningham, Merce. See Merce
   Cunningham Dance Company

Dada, 124
Duchamp, Marcel, 124

Eccles, Andrew, photographs by, 50,
   52–61, 87–92
École de Danse, 124
Evans, Albert, 128–137, 158
"Events" (Cunningham), 19

Fenley, Molissa, 104–5, 158
Folkman, Marjorie, 82–84, 158
Foofwa d'Imobilité, 9, 124–27, 158
Forsythe, William, 86

Gafner, Claude, 124
Gafner, Frédéric. See Foofwa d'Imobilité
Geneva Ballet, 73
Gold, Tom, 86–92, 158
Golden Bowl, The, 73

Jackson, Michael, 73

Katz, Alex, 51
L'Après-Midi d'un Faune (Nijinsky), 69
Le Déjeuner sur l'herbe (Manet), 21
Leite, Ashleigh, 113
Little Ease (Streb), 106–10
Lost, Found, Lost (Taylor), 51–61

Madonna, 73

Man and the Echo, The (Perron), 152
Manet, 21
Marcovici, Sébastien, 128, 158
Martins, Peter, 86
Merce Cunningham Dance Company,
   12–19, 73, 94, 124, 158
Miller, Abbott, 9
Modigliani, 94
Morris, Mark, 26–28, 158

New York City Ballet, 86, 128, 152
New York Dance and Performance
   Award (Bessie), 124
Nijinsky, Vaslav, 69

O Vertigo, 44–48, 159
Ogan, Banu, 94–99, 159
Overgaard, Anders, photographs by,
   95–99

Parker, David, 62–67
Parkinson, Elizabeth, 6
Parsons, David / Parsons Dance
   Company, The, 36–42, 159
Paul Taylor Dance Company, 50–61,
   100–103, 142–51, 159
Perron, Wendy, 152
Petronio, Stephen. See Stephen Petronio
   Dance Company
Prix de Lausanne, 124
Proia, Alexandre, 68–71, 138–41, 159

Rad, Peter, photographs by, 106, 108–10
Rinaldo, Tony, photographs by, 20–25
Robbins, Jerome, 86
Roberts, Keith, 6

Savio, Joanne, photographs by, 44–48
Schoeller, Martin, photographs by, 6,
   8, 9, 26, 36–42, 68, 70–71, 72, 74–77,
   104–5, 123–27, 138–41
School of American Ballet, 152
Sélavy, Rrose, 124
Selya, John, 6
Seven Dances (Taylor), 51
Stephen Petronio Dance Company,
   112–22, 159
Streb, Elizabeth, 106–10, 159
Stuttgart Ballet, 124
Tanner, Richard, 86
Tarr, Patsy, 7
Taylor, Janie, 128, 158
Taylor, Paul. See Paul Taylor Dance
   Company
Tharp, Twyla, 6, 86, 159

Tuttle, Ashley, 6
2wice, 6, 7, 8, 9, 69

Virginia Episcopal School, 142

Westbeth, 19
Witkin, Christian, photographs by,
   12–13, 19–25, 30–35, 62–67, 78–81,
   100–103, 112, 114–22, 129–37,
   143–51, 153–57